CONTENTS

CW00937812

INTRODUCTION   4

DESIGN   8

WORLD WAR I   12
- Naval operations
- The Machine Gun Corps (Motors)
- Gallipoli
- 'They searched the whole world for war'
- The Yeomanry
- India

THE INTERWAR YEARS   23
- An interim design
- The 1920 Pattern cars
- The Royal Air Force
- Ireland
- India
- The 1924 Pattern cars
- Four wheels good – six wheels better

WORLD WAR II   43
- The Home Guard

BIBLIOGRAPHY   47

INDEX   48

THE ROLLS-ROYCE ARMOURED CAR

INTRODUCTION

Rolls-Royce: the hyphenated name has become a byword for top quality; you can buy the Rolls-Royce of lawnmowers, of food processors, whatever you like. One never seems to hear Mercedes-Benz used in the same way. It was ever thus; as early as 1906 members of the War Office Mechanical Transport Committee, attending the Motor Car Show at Olympia in London, were seduced by the quality of a 15hp Rolls-Royce, although they had sense enough to realize that at £525 it was far too expensive for the military budget. It takes a war to justify that.

The first Rolls-Royce armoured car was privately owned. It belonged to a member of the Eastchurch Squadron, Royal Naval Air Service, which in August 1914 was based in Dunkirk. Its commanding officer, Commander Charles Rumney Samson R. N. was something of a firebrand who supplemented his squadron's flying activities by ground-based reconnaissance forays using his pilots' private cars, and these turned into active fighting raids against German patrols operating in the area. As a result of this, and in particular an action at Cassel on 4 September 1914, it was decided to fit armour on to three of these cars, although armour was a relative term. Charles Samson's brother Felix was the prime mover in this project; however, it was up to Charles Samson himself to obtain authority from the Admiralty Air Department in London. The cars selected were Felix Samson's Mercedes, a 50hp Rolls-Royce – which may well have been Charles Samson's own car – and a Wolseley. Work on the cars was undertaken by the Dunkirk shipbuilders Forges et Chantiers de France. Samson admits that the 'armour' was 6mm boiler plate, which was only proof against a rifle bullet above 500 yards. Although Charles Samson states that the protective plate was designed by his brother Felix, the pattern is very similar to that seen on some early Belgian armoured cars with a high, V-shaped shield at the back, and a plate covering the radiator and another around the dashboard. It was armed with a borrowed French Lewis gun to begin with and then a water-cooled Maxim, mounted on a tripod and capable of firing over the rear shield. The Belgians had adopted the practice of reversing towards the enemy, ready for a swift getaway should the need arise. This may well have been the idea behind the British design as well.

The Royal Naval Air Service, as a branch of the Royal Navy, came under the watchful eye of First Lord of the Admiralty Winston Churchill, although Samson's direct superior, as Director of the Admiralty Air Department, was Commodore Murray Sueter. So while Samson experimented with a variety of

NEW VANGUARD • 189

THE ROLLS-ROYCE ARMOURED CAR

DAVID FLETCHER   ILLUSTRATED BY HENRY MORSHEAD

First published in Great Britain in 2012 by Osprey Publishing,
Midland House, West Way, Botley, Oxford, OX2 0PH, UK
43-01 21st Street, Suite 220B, Long Island City, NY 11101, USA
Email: info@ospreypublishing.com

Osprey Publishing is part of the Osprey Group

A CIP catalog record for this book is available from the British Library

Print ISBN: 978 1 84908 580 9

PDF e-book ISBN: 978 1 84908 581 6

EPUB e-book ISBN: 978 1 78096 402 7

Page layout by Melissa Orrom Swan, Oxford
Index by Sharon Redmayne
Typeset in Sabon and Myriad Pro
Originated by PDQ Digital Media Solutions, Suffolk
Printed in China through World Print Ltd.

13 14 15 16   11 10 9 8 7 6 5 4 3

The Woodland Trust
Osprey Publishing is supporting the Woodland Trust, the UK's leading
woodland conservation charity, by funding the dedication of trees.

www.ospreypublishing.com

EDITOR'S NOTE

Main front cover image courtesy of Cody Images. www.codyimages.com

ARTIST'S NOTE

Readers may care to note that the original paintings and the 3D models
from which the colour plates in this book were prepared are available for
private sale. All reproduction copyright whatsoever is retained by the
Publishers. All enquiries should be addressed to:

hmxdesign@tiscali.co.uk

The Publishers regret that they can enter into no correspondence upon this
matter.

AUTHOR'S NOTE

The author would like to thank the following for their kind assistance in the
compilation of this work. Neal Gunderson, John Fasal, Errol Dunne, Karl
Martin and Richard Doherty.

locally built armoured vehicles in Flanders he was urging Sueter, in London, to expand the fleet and inevitably Winston Churchill was interfering. The final number of armoured cars authorised was 60, of which 18 would be Rolls-Royce and 21 each on Wolseley and Clement-Talbot chassis. The design, for some reason, was worked out by the Admiralty Air Department and Lord Wimborne in Britain with no reference to Samson as far as anyone can tell, but the design was submitted to Churchill, who approved it, and a wooden mock-up was created on a real Rolls-Royce chassis to Lord Wimborne's design.

The design did not prove popular with Samson's men because it offered no protection to anyone whose torso projected above the waist-high armour. The only member of the crew to have a seat appears to have been the driver, who was also sheltered to some extent by a steel hood. For the rest of the crew, however, it was necessary to lie down if they found themselves under fire. The sketch submitted to Churchill showed a car with four potential machine-gun mountings around the body although in practice only two appear to have been provided, with the most popular the one on top of the driver's hood. In any case, there was only one Maxim to spare for each car. The armour, such as it was, is described as 4mm nickel chrome steel, lined on the inside with oak planks. There are differences in detail between the various cars. Most had some sort of protection for the tyres, while the radiator was covered by an angled plate, although hinged radiator doors are also seen. Eight cars, probably Talbots and Wolseleys, were built by the Royal Naval Dockyard at Sheerness but subsequently the armour was fitted by each manufacturer at their works, which might account for the differences. The cars were organized into four squadrons, each of 15 cars and with crews largely drawn from the Royal Marines. The first of these, No. 1 Squadron commanded by Lieutenant Felix Samson, was supposed to be equipped entirely with Rolls-Royces. Samson remarks that 'the Rolls-Royces proved by far the most reliable and suitable'. However, it would be wrong to take the orderly arrangement this implies at face value. Flight Commander T.G. Hetherington, who was ordered to join Felix Samson's squadron with four Wolseleys, was horrified by what he found in France. Under Charles Samson anarchy reigned, nobody seemed to know what was going on and organization was non-existent. Evidence

The first three of Commander Samson's armoured cars must have looked like this, although this is the Rolls-Royce showing the additional panels of steel covering the radiator, the driver's position and the machine-gun post at the back. It is also the only one of these three cars that appears to have been photographed.

Samson had one of the original Admiralty Pattern Rolls-Royce cars rebuilt, adding higher sides to protect the crew. It was sometimes seen towing a 47mm gun. Nothing is known about the ultimate fate of the car although Samson later found the gun in Gallipoli and reclaimed it.

suggests that none of the squadrons was ever completed, let alone with the makes of car laid down on paper. Yet it was the British penchant for improvisation at its best, where courage and daring made up for a lack of order and it adds a bright page to an otherwise drab account of a long and depressing war.

Most of the cars underwent modifications in service. Some had planks, carried in brackets on the sides, which could be used to bridge ditches and narrow trenches, while one Rolls-Royce – probably on Samson's orders – had a raised body fitted and was sometimes seen towing a 47mm gun on an improvised two-wheeled carriage. In addition to the 15 Rolls-Royces of No. 1 Squadron, two more are listed as being attached to No. 2 Squadron, which, on paper at least, had 12 Wolseleys. It was the only 14-car squadron of the four, always assuming that any of the squadrons ever reached full strength. But events were moving rapidly, both in terms of technology and on the battlefield.

Writing in Volume 1 of *The World Crisis* Winston Churchill said: 'Thus at the moment when the new armoured-car force was coming into effective existence at much expense and on a considerable scale, it was confronted with an obstacle and a military situation which rendered its employment practically impossible.'

All four squadrons were operational by October 1914 but whether that implies complete to establishment is unclear, and in any case opportunities for action were diminishing rapidly with the creeping expansion of trench warfare. The Admiralty in London was looking at a new design: a turreted car that offered much more protection for the crew. Flight Lieutenant Arthur Nickerson is the man credited with the design of the turret, although the turret itself was by no means a new idea. Turreted armoured cars had existed since about 1904 though they were mostly prototypes, but the idea of the turret goes back further still, to warships and armoured trains. Nickerson, however, created a turret that offered all-round protection with a minimum of weight; unfortunately its curved sides and thin armour with curved plates were not proving easy to produce. Lieutenant Kenneth Symes was working on it but the best results were achieved by Beardmores in Glasgow. The turret armour was 8mm thick, which made it immune to armour-piercing rounds then employed by the Germans.

Even so there was no obvious uniformity. Examination of surviving photographs shows dozens of minor variations in the pattern of the armour and if that were not enough the chassis available differed depending upon the year they were built. This may well have been true of all manufacturers but in the case of Rolls-Royce it has been tabulated in great detail and reveals year-on-year changes with continual minor improvements, so each chassis number needs to be evaluated in this light. For example, chassis produced before 1911 had an exposed drive shaft whereas cars in the 1700 series, produced from 1911 onwards, had the shaft enclosed in a torque tube; chassis produced before 1913 had a three-speed gearbox and from the 1100 series onwards a four-speed box was standard. Unless one knows the chassis number of a particular car this is very difficult to ascertain. As a result it is entirely possible, although by no means certain, that some of the 18 cars earmarked as the first model were completed as the second type, with turrets.

During this time the headquarters of what became the Royal Naval Armoured Car Division (RNACD) had moved from its formative site at the Sheerness naval dockyard on the Isle of Sheppey to the *Daily Mail* airship shed at Wormwood Scrubs in October 1914 although about a month later they left this cold, muddy site for a section of the Clement-Talbot Motor Works facing Barlby Road, North Kensington, less than a mile away to the east. Much of the site was fenced off to enhance security, though this was rather compromised by the open land to the north where it abutted the Great Western Railway. Oddly enough, visitors continued to refer to the site as Wormwood Scrubs and writers still do.

The first turreted Rolls-Royce arrived at the RNACD headquarters at Barlby Road on 15 November 1914, having driven all the way down from Glasgow. More would follow over subsequent months. The armoured car is so familiar and seems to follow the distinctive lines of the classic chassis so precisely that it is difficult to imagine that it could be anything other than a Rolls-Royce. In practice of course there is so little of the original car to see under the armour that some sort of description is essential.

DESIGN

It seems to make sense, under the circumstances, to describe the chassis of these cars and the armoured bodies separately. For one thing, with just a few exceptions, the chassis remained the same on all armoured cars from 1914 until 1925 and minor variations can be dealt with where they occur. The design of armoured hulls, on the other hand, changes dramatically over the years and provides the visual identification features necessary to distinguish one type from another, so they probably need to be treated in greater detail.

Because in those days Rolls-Royce sold only the chassis to their customers, leaving the choice of bodywork to them from a selection of coachbuilders, it was important that the chassis was robust enough to run without a body and, indeed, strong enough to support some of the more ornate bodies, although the company did issue guidelines when it came to weight.

The Silver Ghost chassis had deep, strong side girders braced by five cross-members and at the front by the iconic radiator. Behind the radiator the engine was a straight six, the cylinders grouped in two sets of three with a capacity of 7,428cc with side valves, aluminium alloy pistons and a cast aluminium crankcase. The engine drive passed through a cone clutch to a four-speed and reverse gearbox. In common with many cars of that time both gear lever and handbrake were mounted on the chassis side, to the driver's right, and of course in those days synchromesh was almost unknown and all the gears were

1. ORIGINAL RNAS ROLLS-ROYCE IN FLANDERS 1914

This image is taken from a photograph of a group of Scots Guards with an Admiralty armoured car on the Menin Road on 14 November 1914 during the First Battle of Ypres. In all 18 Rolls-Royce Silver Ghost chassis were earmarked for conversion to what became known as the First Admiralty Pattern armoured cars although whether all of them were ultimately completed in this form is unclear.

Protection was minimal because the armour was too low and too thin to protect the men adequately and the firepower was limited to a naval Maxim machine gun mounted on top of the driver's head cover and rifles carried by the crew.

For a few weeks these cars enjoyed considerable success in the open country between Ypres and the coast but as the main armies fought their way north, digging trenches, spreading wire and ripping up the ground with artillery fire their operational opportunities were severely restricted. This location later became known as Hell Fire Corner.

Also shown is the original Rolls-Royce radiator badge in red, which according to popular rumour changed to black upon the death of Sir Henry Royce in 1933.

2. TURRETED ROLLS-ROYCE OF RNAS, UK, 1915

The classic 1914 turreted Rolls-Royce belonging to a squadron based in the West Country for training. The car is finished overall in khaki green but a splash of colour is added by the large white ensign, flying from a staff attached to the turret. Other features to note are the trumpet of the klaxon horn on the side of the bonnet, the King of the Road acetylene lamp on the rear tray and the two rifles protruding from loopholes in the body. Firing rifles from inside a vehicle such as this would be difficult at the best of times but with a driver and a machine-gunner in place was virtually impossible.

The snarling fox's mask attached to the front of the turret seems to be unique to this car but presumably it summed up the aspirations of the car's commander, once let loose upon the battlefield.

The badge is that of the Royal Naval Armoured Car Division.

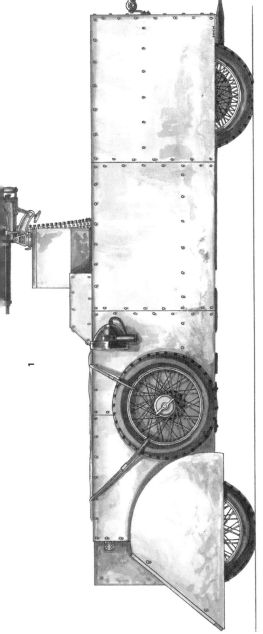

1

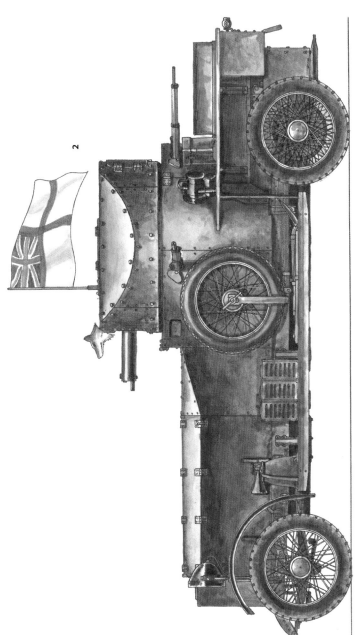

2

This unusual car, photographed in the desert, not only illustrates the difficulties of desert travel but also shows an otherwise undocumented conversion. Either it was a local modification or, just possibly, the previously illustrated Pom-Pom car in a new guise.

square cut, so a skilled driver was taught to double-declutch up and down the box to ensure a smooth gear change. Many less skilled drivers relied on the fact that it was possible to drive the car in top gear in virtually all conditions. However, this could not be done with the weight of an armoured hull on top, so the drivers of these armoured cars were specially trained.

Another novelty, the electric starter motor, was not introduced on the Silver Ghost until 1919. Before that time a car was started on a crank handle through a dual ignition system incorporating two high-tension magnetos and two separate sets of spark plugs on each cylinder. Cars built before 1917 had a trembler coil in the ignition system which could, with luck, be started 'on the switch', although this required some luck and a lot of experience.

Suspension was leaf springs all round, semi-elliptical at the front and cantilever at the back. A footbrake operated on the prop shaft, while the handbrake lever acted on the rear wheels only. By 1913 triple-spoked wire wheels were the most common type, by Dunlop or Rudge-Whitworth. Tyres were Palmer Cord pneumatic, although some armoured cars are seen with the special metal-studded tyres that were supposed to prevent skidding. Fuel was carried in an 18-gallon oval drum at the rear of the chassis delivered under air pressure from a mechanical pump situated at the front or for starting by a hand pump on the dashboard.

For the armoured cars certain modifications were introduced but not necessarily all at the same time. An oil tank, normally located on the left side of the chassis was moved into the engine compartment under armour and a 4-gallon auxiliary fuel tank was also introduced, located in front of the driver. Extra leaves were added to the springs in order to beef up the suspension and twin rims were fitted on the rear axle to spread the weight. Rolls-Royce produced two types of radiator, a standard model and a taller one deemed more suitable for colonial use. This second type was also referred to as the Military version although it was not used on the armoured cars because it would have raised the height of the bonnet armour by about two inches and as a result probably the overall height of the vehicle itself.

The armour plate, as already noted, was 8mm (0.3in.) thick and it enclosed the engine and fighting compartment. At the front two hinged plates acted as protection for the radiator, operated by a long lever from the driver's position; since they interfered with the airflow they would only be closed when the car was under fire and the radiator in danger although they were never entirely airtight. Incidentally, it is worth noting that the wheels and

According to driver Sam Rolls, in *Steel Chariots in the Desert*, it was so hot in the Libyan desert that the men inside the armoured cars 'were in danger of being cooked like rabbits in a saucepan'. As a result 'the turrets were removed when we were on reconnaissance work. The Maxim gun was then fixed in a special mounting which allowed it to be turned in any direction, as in the turret.' Quite how this mounting was arranged is not clear and this poor photograph is the only one we have that appears to show this.

tyres were totally unprotected. This seems odd although in practice wheel damage or punctures from bullets seem to have been rare, while the additional armour only created unnecessary weight. The side panels protecting the engine were secured at the top by wing nuts and could be removed entirely for maintenance. The two top panels were hinged along the centre line but could also be removed if required.

Behind the engine the armour flared out to create the fighting compartment. It was of bolted construction and included a hinged panel for the driver, which could be opened up when it was safe to do so but had a pair of narrow vision slits for use in an emergency and small sliding panels on each side to improve the driver's view right and left. The armour curved round at the back, to roughly the same radius as the turret diameter but with a pair of hinged doors at the very back that provided the only access for the crew to the central compartment. Above this area was the turret. It had curved side plates, with a small hatch at the rear, a flat top plate with another hatch and sloped bevels at each side linking the top and side plates. This arrangement, so distinctive of armoured cars at this time, was clearly done to reduce overall weight, though it made the fighting compartment somewhat cramped when it contained the full crew of three.

The main armament was a water-cooled Maxim of .303-inch calibre, later replaced by the equivalent Vickers weapon as that became available. This protruded through an aperture in the front of the turret, large enough to permit elevation and depression of the weapon but possibly a bit too big to prevent the ingress of enemy rounds, to the detriment of the crew. The machine gun itself was supported in a forked mounting attached to the turret so that elevation, depression and rotation of the turret had to be performed manually by the gunner.

The driver sat on a leather cushion, normally referred to as a squab, on the car's wooden floor with his legs stretched out in front of him and his back supported by a broad leather sling, attached to the side of the car on his right and hooked to the centre of the dashboard on his left. This had to be instantly detachable in the event that the driver had to drive in reverse, still in touch with all the controls but lying partly on his left side and peering out through the rear doors in order to see where he was going.

WORLD WAR I

Naval operations

No sooner had the new turreted cars started to arrive in Flanders than opportunities to use them aggressively began to dry up. Samson himself confessed as much in a report to the Admiralty and before the end of February 1915 he had been recalled to Britain along with his aircraft and most of the armoured cars. Many of those that remained were heavy gun lorries; Seabrooks mostly armed with 47mm (3-pounder) guns serving under the Duke of Westminster, who, although nominally in command of No. 2 Squadron, styled himself 'Officer Commanding Armoured Cars' based at Dunkirk. And although it was true that the 3-pounder guns were more useful in the trenches, for dealing with specific objectives over open sights, the armoured lorries proved much too heavy for the prevailing conditions, often slipping into shell holes and getting stuck. As a result some experiments were conducted by the Duke's force in France, which followed on from work initiated by Samson in the previous year. This took the form of a 3-pounder fitted to an improvised carriage and towed by a Rolls-Royce armoured car. Experiments were being carried out by Lieutenant Anthony Wilding, the New Zealand lawn tennis star, and although the gun proved lighter and much easier to emplace there was some question as to whether even the powerful Rolls-Royce was strong enough to tow it in poor conditions. The RNACD staff at Barlby Road carried out a similar experiment, although the gun carriage they produced was a very solid affair that would have been hard work for a Rolls-Royce, even on good, solid ground.

Petty Officer Sam Rolls, a driver in the Duke of Westminster's No. 2 Squadron, reported that they arrived in Flanders towards the end of March 1915 but that the only work they were given was what he described as 'taxi duty' taking 'brass-hatted messengers' into the forward areas where it was unsafe for an unarmoured staff car to go. He described driving through Ypres, along a road under constant shellfire with a lookout man lying along a front mudguard shouting directions.

The Machine Gun Corps (Motors)

The War Office, somewhat reluctantly, took on the responsibility for the Royal Naval Air Service armoured cars on the Western Front towards the end of 1915 and their first reaction seems to have been to bring them all back to Britain for reorganization. They were incorporated into a special section of the Machine Gun Corps, known as the Machine Gun Corps (Motors) – not to be confused with the Motor Machine Gun Corps, which operated motorcycle

When the army finally did take over many of the armoured cars were defrocked of their armour while others were issued to units engaged in home defence, mainly on the east coast. This pair was issued to the 1/6th (Cyclists) Battalion, the Essex Regiment who proudly emblazoned the regimental title on each car.

Even so a few cars remained in France. This photograph was taken in Arras in April 1917. The car has been camouflage painted, clad in a substance called Uralite for improved protection and has a hook fitted at the front to drag away barbed wire. It is towing a 47mm, 3-pounder gun on an improvised carriage.

machine-gun units, though they were later amalgamated. Those that returned to France were generally organized as Light Armoured Batteries, each of four cars except, for some reason, 7 LAB, which had five. Three of these batteries, 7, 8 and 9, returned to France in March 1916 but found precious little glory. They were attached to the cavalry and employed mostly on liaison duties but, as Samson had already discovered, they were effectively road bound and had few opportunities to advance to where the action was. Attempts were made to employ them on the Somme in 1916 but little evidence for this survives beyond one well-known photograph of a Rolls-Royce escorting an ambulance at a Casualty Clearing Station near Guillemont in September. The car is quite distinctive, with a box-shaped cupola on top of the turret, chains on the rear wheels and no front mudguards but there is no indication as to which unit it belonged to. The Battle of Guillemont spanned four days, 3–6 September, and the casualties were very high. Some ten days later British tanks would roll into action for the very first time.

The Battle of Arras, which began with the German retreat to the Hindenburg Line, included what the Official History describes as a 'skilfully conducted operation' involving elements of the Oxford Light Infantry, 18th Bengal Lancers and two armoured cars, which we assume would be Rolls-Royces, that captured the German-held village of Roisel, east of Peronne on 26 March 1917.

During the main British attack, which was to feature tanks once again, a number of camouflaged Rolls-Royce armoured cars were photographed in the village of Tilloy-les-Mofflaines on the Arras–Cambrai road just east of Arras.

There is no evidence that these cars, when photographed, were doing anything at all but the location places them well forward, up against the front-line trenches of the Hindenburg system waiting for the tanks to achieve a breakthrough so that they could be launched along the Cambrai road. However, up to this time no evidence has been found to coordinate the activities of the armoured cars and tanks so it may be no more than coincidence, and again we have no indication of the units involved.

As it was, all three Light Armoured Batteries had been withdrawn from France by October 1917, so they missed the opportunity to take part in the Battle of Cambrai, for which some people imagine they would have been ideally suited. British armoured cars did not return to the Western Front until the following summer; these, however, were not Rolls-Royces.

North Persia Force (or Norperforce) tested the Rolls-Royce armoured cars to the limit. The cars and their crews came from 15 Light Armoured Motor Battery (LAMB) and those that survived were subsequently incorporated into No. 1 Armoured Car Company, Tank Corps. Norperforce was sent to the Caspian in 1919 to protect the oil installations but was driven out by a Bolshevik invasion in 1920 and had a hard time fighting its way back to Mesopotamia.

His Majesty's Armoured Car *Chatham* belonged to 1st Armoured Car Company, Tank Corps based in Mesopotamia in 1922. Here they practised cooperation with the Royal Air Force and the wireless installation in *Chatham* was installed by the RAF in order to enhance this. Notice that in addition to the aerial mounted on the turret the rear hatch has been modified to open upwards. Notice also the LAMB symbol, still retained on the back of the petrol tank.

Gallipoli

In all eight armoured cars were landed on the peninsula – four each (a section) from Nos. 3 and 4 Squadrons. They were installed in specially prepared dugouts on Helles, without their machine guns, which were used separately. It seems that Commander Josiah Wedgwood MP, commanding No. 3 Squadron, was in charge of the machine guns on board the legendary assault ship *River Clyde*, while the commander of No. 4 Squadron, Lieutenant-Commander James Boothby, was killed at Anzac on 2 May, presumably commanding his machine guns there.

There is only one recorded operation involving the armoured cars on Gallipoli and that was in the battle known variously as Third Krithia or the Battle of the 4th of June (1915). According to the Official History all eight cars were used: 'three roads and tracks leading towards the front line were to be specially bridged beforehand', which may mean the same thing as other accounts that state the tracks were prepared and British trenches filled in, in order to facilitate the advance of the cars. The account published in *Rolls-Royce and the Great Victory* claims that one section fitted its cars out with grapnels at the rear in order to drag away the Turkish wire.

Two eyewitness accounts exist, one from within armoured car Fox and the other from a Chief Petty Officer from the armoured car division who was nearby; both accounts are similar. The advance of the cars was greeted with tremendous cheering from troops nearby but things soon began to go wrong. One car slipped off the road and toppled over, another went over a bump so hard that its turret came off and at least one was so damaged that it turned back. G.V. Sharkey in Fox reported that they came under so much fire the bullets could be heard striking the armour, tyres were shredded and wheels damaged. In fact, the armoured cars were being employed as tanks before these had been designed. It was not a suitable role for armoured cars and it has been suggested that the experiment of fitting an armoured car body to a Killen-Strait tracked tractor in London about a month later was linked to this event.

C.R. Kutz, in *War on Wheels* (Bodley Head, 1941) wrote that all cars were extricated with minor damage and slight casualties. If this is so then the chances are that all eight cars were subsequently removed from Gallipoli later in the year.

Commander Samson, who was with his squadron on Tenedos at the time, felt that if the armoured cars had been used more aggressively at the outset more positive results may have been achieved, but Samson was clearly miffed that his expertise as an armoured car pioneer had been ignored by the authorities at Gallipoli and may well be a biased witness; things had moved on dramatically in a very short time.

'They searched the whole world for war' – *Lieutenant A.G. Stern, RNVR*
While the armoured car squadrons grew apace in London, opportunities to use them in France and Flanders diminished with even greater rapidity, provoking Stern's comment, in the words of an American vaudeville song 'they were all dressed up and nowhere to go'. But the men chosen to command these squadrons were influential, strong-minded characters who used their connections and will power to create opportunities; men such as the Duke of Westminster, Oliver Locker-Lampson MP, Josiah Wedgwood MP and others were able to arrange to take their squadrons to other theatres where opportunities for action seemed greater.

There were in all six squadrons of the RNACD equipped with Rolls-Royce (12 cars each) and three of Lanchesters. Of the former, No. 1 Squadron went to south-west Africa in April 1915, No. 2 went to France and subsequently to Egypt early in 1916, No. 3 went to Egypt in March 1915, No. 4 followed to Egypt in April 1915 (but both squadrons detached a section to the Dardanelles) Nos. 7, 8 and 9 Squadrons went to France.

The changeover from Admiralty to army control seems to have gone smoothly enough in most theatres except, for some reason, for the unit sent to German south-west Africa. It left Britain in March 1915 as No. 1 Squadron, RNAS under the command of Lieutenant-Commander W. Whittall, but since conditions out there were said to be unsuitable for heavy vehicles Whittall left his three Seabrook armoured lorries behind and only took his 12 Rolls-Royce armoured cars. Mobility remained a serious problem, particularly when it was discovered that the armoured cars were using as much water as fuel, and the transport they relied upon to support them either broke down or found the going too tough. However, it was all over by July 1915 when the Germans surrendered and the squadron was ordered home.

In the meantime events in East Africa threatened to run on endlessly so it was agreed that a section of four cars, under Lieutenant Nalder, should be transferred there from Whittall's squadron.

Whittall joined them a few months later and they were designated 10th (Royal Naval) Armoured Motor Battery, which suggests that the men did not wish to transfer to the army or that there were insufficient trained army personnel to replace them. Either way the unit was transferred to Egypt in January 1917 and disbanded.

If the African jungle presented terrible handicaps to the armoured cars, not to mention other vehicles, the vast expanse of sand and rock that constitutes the deserts covering north Africa, Arabia and the countries now known as Iran and Iraq was also a dramatic challenge. And yet somehow one tends to associate Rolls-Royce armoured cars with this blasted wasteland, as if it were their spiritual home.

The first of these to grab public recognition was the Light Armoured Car Brigade of three batteries commanded by the Duke of Westminster, now wearing the uniform of a Major of the Cheshire Yeomanry, operating in the Western Desert based at Mersah Matruh. In fact the operation that brought the Duke and his force to the notice of the British public was the rescue of the crew of HMS *Tara* in March 1916, accomplished by a 300-mile round trip deep into the desert that resulted in the rescue of 91 British prisoners, all of whom were on the verge of dying of starvation.

A few days prior to this the armoured cars had scored a remarkable victory over their enemies, the Senussi, by demonstrating how the mechanized vehicles, even in such harsh conditions, had rendered the old Arab habit of simply melting away into the desert untenable with this new combination of firepower, mobility and protection. This is believed to have been the largest combat operation involving armoured vehicles up to that time.

It was a detachment, initially of two cars, from the Duke's Light Armoured Car Brigade along with two from East Africa, which formed the original Hedjaz Section that operated with Lawrence of Arabia in support of Sherif Hussein and his Arab Revolt. Much of what he achieved was clearly due to Lawrence's personality and his ability to hold the tribes together but one imagines that some of the weapons he was able to conjure, in particular the aircraft and armoured cars, also impressed the irregulars. Lawrence

B

1. TURRETED ROLLS-ROYCE OF THE MACHINE GUN CORPS (MOTORS) WESTERN FRONT 1917

A number of Rolls-Royces were still serving on the Western Front in April 1917, at the time of the Battle of Arras, but there are very few accounts of their activities. Two of the cars were seen parked up in the village of Tilloy-les-Mofflaines, on the Cambrai road. By this time the army had put its imprint on them and many of the cars had a raised cupola on the turret roof, a shield for the machine gun and a hinged hook at the front for dragging away barbed wire. Many were clad in a mineral substance known as Uralite, which it was hoped would absorb the impact of bullets before they reached the armour.

Some of the cars were finished in an irregular three-tone camouflage scheme but, since the actual colours were not recorded, the best one can say for this rendition is that it is an educated guess. Although tanks were operating in the area at this time there is no evidence of any cooperation between them and indeed British armoured cars were withdrawn from the Western Front not long after this, not to return until the Austins of 17th Battalion, Tank Corps in June 1918.

The badge is that of the Machine Gun Corps, which both armoured car and tank crews would have worn at this time.

2. TURRETED ROLLS-ROYCE IN MIDDLE EAST c.1915

Armoured cars operating in desert regions, whether with the Royal Naval Air Service or the Machine Gun Corps are often seen in photographs with the upper panels of armour removed from the turret and above the engine. It may not have reduced the heat but at least it improved the airflow for both the crew and the engine. In terms of vulnerability, since there was no threat from the air at this time the modification makes sense, but compare this with the car depicted in Plate F.

Crews were rapidly learning the art of self-sufficiency as they roamed deeper into this inhospitable land. Water, of course, for the car first, then the crew; spare tyres to replace those shredded on the harsh surface; and stout tow ropes and chains permanently attached. Notice the folded tripod for the machine gun strapped to the running board.

The insignia is that of a LAMB, or Light Armoured Motor Battery, as seen later in the war, accompanied by a metal arm badge, depicting a Rolls-Royce armoured car as issued in the Middle East.

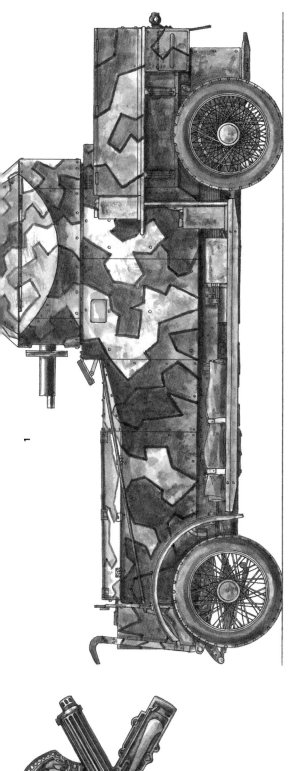

1

2

'Scotland for Ever' Is emblazoned on the side of this car along with the LAMB symbol typical of armoured cars in the Middle East later in the war. The standing figure is clearly from a Scottish regiment. Notice the spare tyres stacked on top of the turret and the protective sacking wrapped around the machine gun.

himself clearly enjoyed this form of warfare although Sam Rolls, one of his drivers, reckoned that for efficient operation only two men should be inside the turret: the driver and a machine-gunner. At such times the driver assisted the gunner by feeding ammunition belts to him with his free hand.

Given the space available it is impossible to follow the adventures of all the armoured cars in this region so for a flavour it seems best to single out three. It was a car from 13th LAMB that rescued Colonel John Tennant and Major P.R.C. Hobart from captivity after their plane was brought down, with Hobart, of course, later to become famous as the commanding officer of 79th Armoured Division in World War II, and it was 14th LAMB, commanded by Captain Nigel Somerset (grandson of Lord Raglan of Crimean fame) that had as one of its officers the American Kermit Roosevelt, son of former President Theodore Roosevelt. By 1919 14th LAMB was operating in Kurdistan and a year later its armoured cars and those crew members not immediately due for demobilization were absorbed into the Tank Corps as No. 2 Armoured Car Company.

Doyen of them all however was 15th LAMB, which had been created in Egypt in July 1917. It also served in Mesopotamia until the end of the war but then became part of North Persia Force (Norperforce) in 1919, which involved a deep incursion into Persia towards the Russian oilfields on the

The Hedjaz Section, which served with Lawrence of Arabia, included four Rolls-Royces that had been transferred from the Libyan Desert. Here are three of them, fitted with double rims on the front axle, which may have been popular when crossing soft sand but not, perhaps, with anyone who had to steer them. All three cars have their turrets reversed.

This photograph, taken at Al Mayadin on the Euphrates in January 1919, shows Rolls-Royce armoured cars of 6th LAMB, finished in a very exotic camouflage scheme, on internal security duties. The car nearest the camera is one of a small batch produced at the end of the war with enlarged turrets. Compare with the lower-sided turret of the car in the background.

Caspian Sea. It was a harsh test for both cars and men but it seems that the Allies had underestimated the Bolsheviks, who in due course drove them out of the region. The cars and men of 15th LAMB were also absorbed by the Tank Corps in 1920 and became No. 1 Armoured Car Company.

The Yeomanry

A number of Yeomanry regiments acquired armoured cars during World War I but only one, so far as surviving records show, obtained a Rolls-Royce. The Yeomanry was essentially volunteer cavalry, raised originally from rural society in the late eighteenth century to protect the country from invasion. By 1914 it was attracting the fashionable elite and had already established official authority to fight alongside the British Army overseas. The acquisition of an armoured car, often before the War Office had shown any interest in the subject, not only helped to prove the forward thinking outlook of the regiment but also served as a useful recruiting tool in its local area.

The elegant Rolls-Royce, with an armoured body by the London coachbuilders Barker & Company, was obtained by the Scottish Horse Yeomanry Regiment although the armoured car probably remained in Scotland while the regiment went overseas, initially to the Mediterranean theatre.

Military interest at this time seems to have been limited to the Yeomanry, who purchased their own vehicles. This car was owned by the Scottish Horse, a Perthshire regiment who are the only ones known to have employed a Rolls-Royce with a body by the London coachbuilders Barker & Company.

India

Captain Anthony Clifton liked to describe himself as an officer of 'the old 68th' (the 68th Foot, that is) although they had been known as the Durham Light Infantry since 1881. Yet for all his quaint, archaic ways he was a very modern young officer who had served for some time with the Army Service Corps. He was convinced that mechanical transport was the answer to the problems of supply in India, most particularly on the North

The first armoured cars to appear in India were designed and assembled locally. Three of them were on Rolls-Royce chassis and proved to be the most reliable. They operated as 1st Armoured Motor Battery, based in Peshawar, and spent virtually all of their time on the North West Frontier. The battery was commanded by Captain A.J. Clifton, Durham Light Infantry.

West Frontier, and he also appreciated that some sort of protected vehicle might be useful.

In later years Clifton gave the impression that he was the only instigator of armoured cars in India although as a lowly captain his opinion did not carry much weight with the Viceroy, Lord Hardinge. Fortunately there was someone of far greater influence in India who agreed with Clifton. This was Lord (John) Montague of Beaulieu, who was appointed Inspector of Mechanical Transport for India in April 1915. He was a staunch believer in mechanical transport of all kinds and could immediately see the possibilities of what were then called armoured motors.

Out of 38 armoured motors in India in 1915 only three were on Rolls-Royce chassis. Clifton wrote that even where chassis were of the same make they were never of the same year or model; in the case of the Rolls-Royce they must all have been of the 40/50hp type although, as we have seen, these

C

1. LOCALLY PRODUCED ROLLS-ROYCE ARMOURED CAR IN INDIA c.1915

Three Rolls-Royces were among the first armoured cars (or armoured motors as they were known out there) built in India, although the term 'armoured' was something of an exaggeration. A.J. Clifton, the officer who designed and commanded them, said that the metal plate used was hardly sufficient to stop a rifle bullet, even at point-blank range.

One in three cars was intended to carry a vintage Maxim machine gun and was fitted with rounded bays at each side to give the gunner more room to swing the weapon round. Clifton not only commanded the armoured motors and produced a small booklet on tactical use and training (in 1917), he even worked out an ideal camouflage scheme, a mixture of light khaki and dark green as shown here.

Also shown is the black and silver embroidered Topee Flash worn by members of No. 1 Armoured Motor Unit.

2. TURRETED ROLLS-ROYCE OF NO. 2 RAF ARMOURED CAR COMPANY, IRAQ

The Royal Air Force acquired about two dozen Rolls-Royce armoured cars, some from the army and some newly built. The car shown here is an original 1914 Pattern hull, mounted on a new chassis, probably inherited from the Machine Gun Corps in 1923. It exhibits various modifications introduced by the RAF, which included a spotlight on the turret, a Lewis gun at the back and holders for furled flags on the turret bevels.

The car has the RAF cockade on the side, and in front of the driver and the name, painted in white on the side panel of the bonnet, is HMAC (His Majesty's Armoured Car) *Cheetah*. By 1940 the majority of these armoured hulls had been transferred to Fordson (British-built Ford commercial) chassis, probably the 30cwt four-wheeler powered by a Ford V-8 engine.

The smaller image is the badge of the Royal Air Force as it would have been at that time.

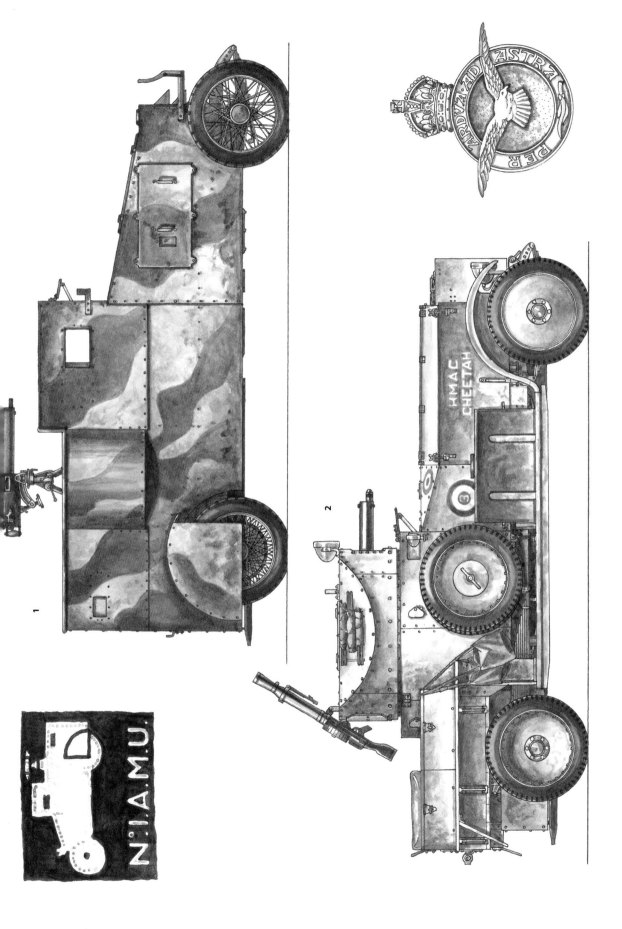

1

2

N·I·A·M·U·

HMAC CHEETAH

One of the three improvised Rolls-Royce cars in India, number 2641, was ultimately rebuilt locally as a turreted armoured car and for much of its long career rejoiced in the name of *Wedding Bells*. It is seen here alongside *Dana*, a Crossley armoured car of a more typical Indian pattern. *Wedding Bells* was virtually derelict by 1940 and was ultimately scrapped in about 1948, but legends concerning its career in World War II are largely fiction.

changed on a more or less yearly basis. Their origins are shrouded in mythology but it seems clear enough that these were civilian-style chassis not specially prepared for armoured car work. The armour, such as it was, was to a design worked out by Clifton and fitted at the workshops of the various Indian railway companies. Clifton said that he once fired a rifle bullet at some of the so-called armour plate and that it went right through – information that he prudently decided to keep to himself.

Since machine guns were scarce in India at this time only one could be spared per three cars and this affected the design. Each car had steel plates covering the engine and radiator and a short roof above the driver. Otherwise the body of each car was a high-sided box, open at the top and with a door at the back. The machine gun was mounted on a pedestal in the centre of the floor and the dedicated machine-gun car had bowed-out sides to enable the gunner to swing the weapon round. The other two cars were flat sided and contained seats for riflemen. In due course more machine guns were acquired and fitted to all of the cars although Clifton said that they were all rather top heavy and rolled alarmingly.

The three Rolls-Royces formed No. 1 Armoured Motor Unit, which was commanded by Clifton himself and saw action on the North West Frontier, from its base in Peshawar, for the rest of the war. Just like those before him Clifton soon found that the Rolls-Royces were so much more robust and reliable than any other make that he tended to use them turn and turn about with different crews to obtain maximum operational efficiency. Although they were regarded with a good deal of cautious amusement at first, Clifton claims that critics soon came to realize that an Armoured Motor Unit had the mobility of a squadron of cavalry and the firepower of a battalion of infantry – a welcome asset on the frontier that had been denuded of experienced troops to meet the demands from more active fronts.

One of these cars, built on to a 1911 chassis, was rebuilt in 1919 with an enclosed body and rotating turret. The new armour was designed by Clifton's men and fitted by the Gun Carriage Factory at Jubbulpore. For a while in this form it bore the name *Golden Goblin* but in 1920 was rechristened *Wedding Bells*, having acted as the bridal coach at a military wedding. The

hull and turret were subsequently redesigned and the vehicle was not actually reduced to scrap until 1948.

THE INTERWAR YEARS

An interim design

Sometime in 1918 a few more Rolls-Royce armoured cars were produced in Britain, probably no more than five or six, which were identical to the original cars except that they had enlarged turrets, higher at the sides presumably to provide more headroom. They appear to have been assembled by small concerns in Glasgow, garages and coachbuilders primarily, presumably on account of their proximity to Beardmores, one of the main suppliers of armour plate.

Up to the present time only one of these vehicles has been identified in service, with 6th LAMB in Iraq in 1919.

The 1920 Pattern cars

It was generally accepted that in order to come up with a design for a new model of Rolls-Royce armoured car after the war the War Office approached the Admiralty and took copies of the plans they had for the 1914 Pattern cars. However, recent evidence suggests that it was not quite as simple as that. The War Office certainly made an approach but they were told that the Admiralty did not have any drawings because they had placed all the responsibility for this work with a firm called Duff, Morgan and Vermont. They were a Norwich-based firm involved in the automobile industry, and they opened a drawing office in London where the work could be done in close consultation with the navy.

Quite why such an apparently obscure firm should be given this task is not clear, although the answer might be in the name. Messrs Duff and Morgan were local businessmen but Vermont was not. Indeed there never was a Mr Vermont. In those days persons of a certain social standing were rather coy about having their names associated with trade and therefore adopted a pseudonym. In this case the individual concerned, rather than use his own

A few original 1914 Pattern turreted armoured cars ultimately found their way to India via the Middle East from about 1917 onwards. These two are serving with 7th Armoured Car Company, the personnel for which left Dorset in 1920 and arrived in India in February 1921. Based at Peshawar they operated mainly on the North West Frontier. The raised armoured cover on top of the turret was one of many designs and would have proved useful in the Frontier passes.

D ROLLS-ROYCE 1920 PATTERN MARK I

It is virtually impossible to illustrate a typical 1920 Pattern car since they seem to have differed in many details and to have changed as time went by. We have therefore elected to base this drawing on the Tank Museum's exhibit F247, original registration H3830, chassis number 193 WO, with the caution that it has undergone a number of modifications in a long life and therefore should perhaps not be taken as typical.

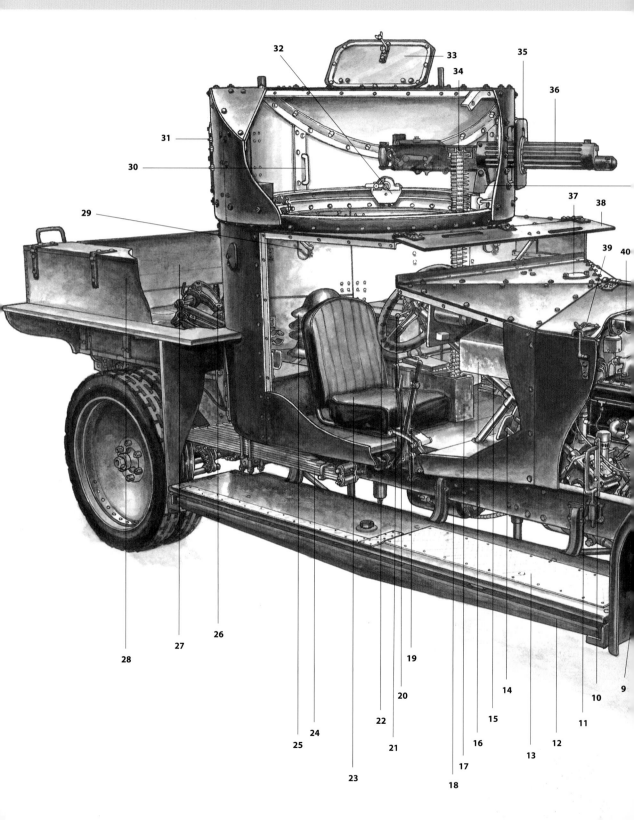

Technical Data

Crew:	2/3	**Maximum speed:**	60 mph
Weight:	3.8 tons	**Radius of action:**	180 miles
Dimensions:	Overall length: 16 ft 7 ins	**Fuel consumption:**	approx. 12 miles per gallon
	Overall width: 6 ft 3 ins	**Trench-crossing ability:**	8 ft 4 ins (with ditching beams)
	Overall height: 7 ft 7 ins	**Armour thickness:**	8mm
	Wheelbase: 11 ft 11.5 ins	**Armament:**	Vickers .303-inch water-cooled machine-gun Mark I, infantry pattern
Engine:	Rolls-Royce 40/50 six cylinder in-line water-cooled dual ignition. 65 bhp at 2,250 rpm; 7.428cc		
		Muzzle velocity:	2,440 feet per second
Transmission:	Through internal, fabric lined cone clutch. Four speed and reverse gearbox – direct drive in fourth	**Rate of fire:**	500 rounds per minute
		Maximum range:	2,900 yards
Fuel capacity:	18 gallons (main tank); 4 gallons (Gravity tank)	**Ammunition:**	.303-inch Mark VII ball cartridge
		Ammunition stowage:	6,000 rounds

Key

1. Armoured radiator door
2. Front towing shackle
3. Starting handle
4. Front spring
5. Front lower armour
6. Palmer Cord tyre
7. Michelin disc wheel
8. Induction pipe
9. Carburettor
10. Bonnet securing handle
11. Steering box
12. Unditching board
13. Running board
14. Foot pedals
15. Steering column
16. Gravity petrol tank
17. Machine-gun ammunition box
18. Dynamo
19. Hand brake lever
20. Gear selector
21. Ignition levers
22. Steering wheel
23. Driver's seat (as fitted to the preserved vehicle)
24. Rear springs
25. Crew helmets
26. Machine-gun tripod
27. Tail gate
28. Stowage locker
29. Pistol port
30. Turret turning handle
31. Turret rear hatch
32. Turret roller
33. Turret top hatch
34. Machine-gun ammunition belt
35. Machine-gun shield
36. Vickers .303 inch machine-gun
37. Petrol filler for gravity tank
38. Hinged visor panel
39. Bonnet securing point
40. Klaxon horn
41. Machine-gun mounting
42. Bonnet top hinge
43. Coolant pipe
44. Radiator doors lever arm
45. Rolls-Royce 40/50hp engine
46. Distributor
47. Radiator
48. Headlamp
49. Radiator door louvres
50. Chassis dumb iron

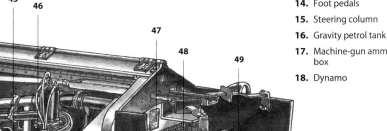

The interior of a 1920 Pattern car readily identified by the different height of the two vision slits in the driver's visor. It is particularly spartan inside with nothing but a rough cushion to sit on and a very basic dashboard. The handbrake and gear change levers can be seen to the right of the steering wheel and the device in the foreground is part of the internal starting device. On the left is the magneto.

name, picked that of his mother's home state, she being an American lady. In real life she was Mrs Locker-Lampson and it was her son, Oliver Locker-Lampson who was 'Vermont'. Whether today the idea that a man who was a Member of Parliament (for North Huntingdonshire) and an officer of the Royal Naval Volunteer Reserve should be involved in this way might raise eyebrows, but in 1915 presumably this was perfectly normal. Locker-Lampson himself is better known as the commander of the expedition to Russia, raised by the Royal Naval Air Service, which was equipped largely with Lanchester armoured cars, supplemented by just one Rolls-Royce.

There are a number of key features that distinguish the 1920 Pattern cars from the wartime model although there are some hybrids that can confuse the issue. The most obvious is the larger, higher-sided turret although as we have seen a few of these turrets appear on earlier cars however, one almost foolproof feature is the driver's hinged visor plate. On a 1914 Pattern the two vision slits for the driver and his mate are on the same level whereas on the 20 Pattern cars the slot in front of the driver is at a higher level than the other.

Disc wheels by Michelin, as distinct from wire spoked wheels, are another good guide although, of course, where a new chassis has been provided for an older car there is some potential for confusion. In that case check out the turret, which should be an infallible guide in conjunction with the wheels. The 20 Pattern cars also carry additional plates attached to the radiator doors, with two slots in each to provide additional airflow when the doors are closed. These were a standard feature but since examples have been seen on earlier cars they need to be treated with caution and only used in conjunction with other features.

Finally the front mudguards or wings should be looked at carefully. Those normally fitted to the 20 Pattern cars appear to be of stronger construction and somewhat shapelier than the basic 14 Pattern but one does see others, which look as if they might have been taken from civilian cars and again these should be studied with some care. Beyond that there are any number of detail modifications and alterations that as far as possible are covered in the photographs.

The total number of Rolls-Royce armoured cars built for the War Office seems to be 77, along with 11 chassis used for instruction purposes. Of these, 24 were of the improved 1924 Pattern so production of the 1920 Pattern, excluding those built for the RAF and of course the special design for India,

works out at 53. Ten of these, however, appear to have been upgraded at some stage and designated 1920 Pattern Mark IA. Quite when this was done is unclear, though it may have been as late as 1933, which is when an example was tested at Farnborough. Coincidentally at around the same time a 1920 Pattern car (M271) was also tested there, fitted with a 100hp Rolls-Royce Phantom engine that, according to some sources, was evaporatively cooled.

Photographs of the Mark IA type are rare but just for the record they featured the Vickers machine gun in a ball mount, like the 1924 Pattern cars; a turret cupola, again like the 1924 Pattern but in this case set longitudinally on top of the turret; and strips of steel, described as anti-splash rails, arranged herringbone fashion on top of the bonnet. Their purpose was to deflect and break up incoming rounds away from the driver's vision slit.

The service record of the 1920 Pattern cars is too long and varied to be covered here in any detail. Some were stationed in Britain: at Bovington, of course, at Warrington and ultimately with eight armoured car companies created from Yeomanry regiments in a post-1918 reorganization. Of course by this time the Yeomanry had returned to its voluntary, part-time soldier role, which normally had two armoured cars on the strength and borrowed others to make up numbers for their annual camp. These were not all Rolls-Royces but whatever they were the normal practice was for the Royal Tank Corps to supply regular soldiers as drivers rather than leaving the cars entirely to the tender mercies of the volunteers. A section of Rolls-Royces, originally from 12th Armoured Car Company, formed part of the occupation forces in Germany, not finally departing from Wiesbaden until 1929.

Two companies of armoured cars amounting to some 20 vehicles in all and mostly, if not all, Rolls-Royces were attached as a reconnaissance element to 3rd Battalion Royal Tank Corps for the Experimental Mechanized Force

Although it may look quite normal at first sight this 1920 Pattern Rolls-Royce carries an experimental air-cooled Vickers machine gun. The slotted panels on the radiator doors are also typical of the later cars, to ensure at least some air reached the radiator even when they are closed.

Known somewhat irreverently as 'the ice-cream cart' this turretless 1920 Pattern car was apparently operated by the commanding officer of No. 3 Armoured Car Company Royal Tank Corps in Egypt. An ugly aerial array has replaced the turret but perhaps an element of vanity or status required that the front-end armour be removed to reveal the Rolls-Royce radiator and a conventional bonnet fitted.

of 1927. Moving swiftly and almost silently down country roads and leafy lanes they rapidly seized virtually every strategic crossing point on the map, denying them to the unmechanized opposition and leaving them prey to the advancing tanks and motorized artillery. It was a glaring exposition of the advantages of mechanization, conducted in full view of the press, but it had budgetary implications that worried the government and posed a threat in the minds of many traditionally minded soldiers. But the exercise was all about tanks, which had captured the public imagination, not about armoured cars, although in practice they had already achieved more than the tanks.

The majority of the new cars were issued to armoured car companies in the Middle East, apart from those hurried over to Ireland, which were originally destined for Mesopotamia. Here, effectively in the tyre tracks of their wartime predecessors they achieved miracles, albeit out of sight of the British public. In Egypt a company of Rolls-Royces went to the Duke of Westminster's old hunting ground at Sollum, while others patrolled in Alexandria and Cairo, even going as far afield as the Sudan, as their predecessors had done in 1915.

The most exciting adventure undertaken by Rolls-Royce armoured cars at this time concerned 5th Armoured Car Company, which had been raised in Ireland and subsequently stationed at Warrington in Cheshire. They sailed from Britain in early 1927 as part of the Shanghai Defence Force and landed

From about 1920 onwards new chassis started to arrive in the Middle East to which the original bodies were transferred. They are easily recognised by the Michelin disc wheels. M350 was a typical War Department number from the early postwar period, which is annotated *chassis only* in a contemporary ledger. The wooden bench seats would be a temporary addition.

An atmospheric photograph taken in Shanghai in 1927. The cars belong to 5th Armoured Car Company, Royal Tank Corps and the two leading ones feature the hinged cupola, nicknamed the 'Top Hat', which gave the commander additional protection.

in China in March. China was then in the throes of a civil war and the Defence Force was there to protect British lives in the international trading community in Shanghai. Their duties were mainly peacekeeping, patrolling and covering road blocks although they did see some action. The cars were modified in China by the fitting of front bumper bars for use in busy traffic and by armoured head covers on the turrets that were known as 'top hats'.

The company left China in January 1929 but got no further than Egypt, where they landed in February. Their role at this time was largely instructional, in particular teaching driving and maintenance skills to men of the 12th Royal Lancers, who were in the process of converting from a horsed cavalry regiment to a mechanized one. They duly inherited the 5th's armoured cars and for the next ten years exchanged stations with their comrades in the 11th Hussars, then stationed in Britain, who were undergoing the same process.

The Royal Air Force

With the drawdown from war and the steady demise of the Machine Gun Corps it was agreed that the armoured cars should now come under the auspices of the Tank Corps. A logical move but not an easy one in such straitened times. The first priority was Iraq, for which Britain held the League of Nations mandate. However, before this could be effected a rebellion broke out and the ridiculous situation arose where the surviving armoured cars had to be crewed by the infantry while the newly arrived Tank Corps people, mostly drawn from the old 4th Tank Battalion, were issued with rifles and posted as infantry to defend Baghdad.

Once the situation calmed down, in January 1921, the Tank Corps was able to reclaim the cars from which, in due course, they created three armoured car companies, the 1st, 2nd and 6th from their own resources along with surviving men and vehicles of 6th and 15th LAMB, and the 7th, 8th and 14th Light Armoured Batteries. But the armoured cars were still

Turret detail of a 1920 Pattern car in Royal Air Force Service. It is unusual in that there is a Lewis gun in the main turret mounting, another one on top of the turret along with a spotlight, and signal flag holders very typical of an RAF car.

Cooperation between armoured cars and aircraft was pioneered by the Tank Corps in Iraq in 1922. Here two 1920 Pattern cars, with twin front wheels, meet up with a pair of Vickers bombers. Armoured cars were also used to mark out the course of the 'All Red Air Route' in this region.

suffering from their poor showing in the Mesopotamian rebellion and in order to restore the situation Lieutenant-Colonel George Lindsay, a Machine Gun Corps pioneer now transferred to the Tank Corps, was sent out in June 1921 to take overall command, which included close cooperation between the armoured cars and the Royal Air Force.

This had far-reaching repercussions. At a conference in London in December 1921 Sir Hugh Trenchard, head of the RAF, backed up by Colonel T.E. Lawrence (of Arabia) advocated total control of Iraq from the air. This suited Trenchard, who was anxious to find a peacetime role for the RAF but it also became clear that they would need armoured cars for control on the ground and, rather than test inter-service cooperation to destruction, it was agreed that the RAF should raise its own Armoured Car Companies and take over the responsibility for Iraq, Palestine and Aden.

To begin with the RAF inherited armoured cars from the Tank Corps, most of which were ex-Machine Gun Corps vehicles of the 1914 Pattern but pending the delivery of new cars many of these received new chassis, resulting in the hybrid 1914/1920 variety also seen in War Office service. In due course the RAF acquired new armoured cars, based on the design of the War Office 1920 Pattern but classified by the RAF as Type A. All told, as far as surviving records show,

At first the RAF managed on 1914 Pattern cars taken over from the army, like this one, known as *Pathfinder*, which has a large electric spotlight on the turret and new front mudguards but is otherwise unmodified.

the total number of Rolls-Royces operated by the RAF was 24, of which 11 were inherited War Office cars and 13 newly built with chassis from Derby and bodies produced by the Royal Ordnance Factory at Woolwich. However, delivery seems to have been in small batches because the last seven did not reach their units until 1927.

The RAF seem to have been quite satisfied with the 1920 design, since there is no evidence that they ever adopted the 1924 Pattern, but they definitely put their own stamp

His Majesty's Armoured Car Python is an unusual vehicle to see in RAF service. It has the longitudinal turret cupola, ball mounting for the Vickers gun and the anti-splash strips on the bonnet that were typical of a 1920 Pattern Mark IA in army service. Being naturally air-minded, the RAF normally had something visible from above either on the bonnet or turret top, but nothing can be seen here.

on these vehicles. Extra machine guns were a common feature, along with fittings for a spotlight and signal flags on the turret, and in particular large section desert tyres on military-style split rims. However, one of their more bizarre applications involved two primitive tracked vehicles, known as Dragons, which were fitted with armoured cabs and supplied to the RAF in order to be fitted with the body and turret of a Rolls-Royce armoured car, which, when required, could be used as a rudimentary tank on ground over which the armoured cars could not operate.

The primary Rolls-Royce user in the RAF was No. 2 Armoured Car Company. It was based in Palestine when, in 1936, a major confrontation developed between Jewish and Arab elements and the army had to be called in to bolster British forces. These included the 11th Hussars with their Rolls≠Royces, many of which were 1924 Pattern but, following the example of the RAF, they removed the cupolas from some of these vehicles and added external Lewis guns to the turret.

Meanwhile, as a new war loomed, the RAF attempted to stretch the life of its older cars by switching the original bodies on to more up-to-date Fordson chassis, fitting an extra crew compartment at the back and enhancing the armament. However, it seems that a few original Rolls-Royces

This car, in pristine condition, is a 1914-style body and turret on a new chassis with split rims and large section desert tyres. The wooden lockers have been redesigned, the headlamps relocated and a spotlight mounted on the front of the turret. Although not shown here it was common practice to paint a large red, white and blue cockade on top of the turret.

remained because one was photographed near Tobruk in about 1941, being inspected by General Rommel after it had been knocked out. This car is believed to be from No. 2 Armoured Car Company RAF, which for a time was acting as D Squadron, 11th Hussars in the Western Desert. This particular car mounts a .55-inch Boys anti-tank rifle to the right of the Vickers gun, something that they had already done with their Fordsons.

Ireland

Seven Rolls-Royce armoured cars were sent across to Ireland in May 1916 in the aftermath of the Easter Rising and it is believed that crews were drawn from the infantry. From then until the end of World War I and some months afterwards they attempted to keep the lid on Republican aspirations. Many of the actions were surprise attacks and ambushes, which only the armoured cars could be expected to deal with. It was a situation that was typical of what the British would have regarded as sideshows, where armoured cars, with their mobility and firepower, replaced the valuable men so desperately needed on the Western Front.

As the war ended and the soldiers returned home, Republican organizations were able to recruit experienced soldiers so the British retaliated and upped the ante. In January 1919 17th (Armoured Car) Battalion of the Tank Corps was swiftly transferred from the occupation forces in Germany to Dublin. New

E

1. ROLLS-ROYCE INDIAN PATTERN, 9TH ARMOURED CAR COMPANY ROYAL TANK CORPS c.1925

The highly distinctive Indian Pattern armour first applied to 19 Rolls-Royce Silver Ghost chassis was also largely A.J. Clifton's design. The dome-shaped turret was considered ideal for operating in the passes of the North West Frontier, where ambushes were often delivered from above, and each car carried two Vickers machine guns for which four mountings were provided. It was possible to switch a gun from one mounting to another in about 15 seconds and cars are often seen in photographs with one gun pointing in each direction. The turret rotated in the normal way but the car commander also had a small, independently rotating cupola on top of the turret, which opened out like a clamshell providing him with some additional protection while scanning his immediate area.

Although this car is finished in a camouflage scheme that seems to adhere to Clifton's principles this did not last long on the frontier where the extreme heat led commanders to prefer white or silver/grey shades that would reflect the sun's rays. Typical of heavy vehicles in India at this time this is fitted with patent Normal Air Pressue (NAP) pneumatic tyres, which were in fact solid rubber with small air pockets cut into them.

The other illustrations are the pennant of the 9th Armoured Car Company, as flown from the commander's vehicle, and the cap badge of the Royal Tank Corps, a miniature of which was worn on the solar topee.

2. ROLLS-ROYCE 1924 PATTERN MARK I 12TH LANCERS, EGYPT 1932

Among the cars that accompanied A Squadron 12th Lancers on their desert expedition to Siwa Oasis in 1932 *Albuera* is the only one, as far as we know, that was finished in this remarkable camouflage scheme. Photographs suggest that the others were in dark green. The A Squadron cars all carried the names of famous battles beginning with A although Albuera (a battle from the Peninsular War in Spain) was not in fact a 12th Lancers' battle honour.

Albuera was seen on another occasion with the disruptive pattern applied only to upper facing surfaces but whether this was before or after the Siwa Expedition is not clear. Two features that distinguish the 1924 Pattern cars, if the turret cannot be seen, are the bulge in the armour in front of the driver's position, which covers the steering wheel, and the fact that the visor itself, instead of being one piece, is split down the middle so that each half can be opened independently.

The other illustration shows the cap badge of the 12th Lancers.

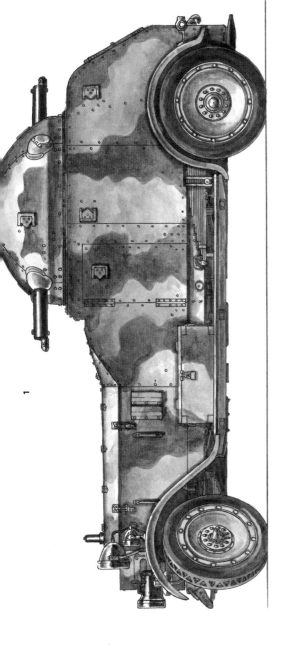

1

2

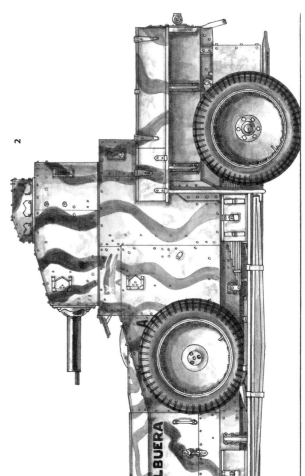

An early example of a 1920 Pattern car on British service in Dublin. The crew all carry revolvers but not steel helmets, which can be a nuisance inside a car. As with most of these cars when they were first built, the ditch-crossing boards are stowed on edge at each side.

Rolls-Royce armoured cars, which should have been destined for Mesopotamia, were sent to Dublin instead to replace a motley collection of other armoured cars in the hands of what was now 5th Armoured Car Company, which had been created from the old 17th Battalion in March 1920.

A truce, agreed in July 1921, and the creation of the Free State the following December, did not bring the conflict to an end; nor did it result in an immediate withdrawal of British forces but in due course the British withdrew to the north, handing over 13 Rolls-Royce armoured cars among over 1,000 other vehicles, which were then taken over by the Irish National Army. Meanwhile the 5th Armoured Car Company moved from Dublin to Belfast where it was subsequently replaced by 12th Armoured Car Company in April 1922. However they were recalled across the Irish Sea in May 1926 and based at Warrington in Cheshire during the British General Strike. The Royal Ulster Constabulary received six 1920 Pattern cars from a vast depot and airfield maintained by the British Army at Gormanston Camp in Eire. These patrolled the border with the Republic during World War II, often opposite similar cars in service with the Irish National Army. At such times the cars each flew their nation's flags.

The 13 cars handed over to the Irish National Army included 12 1920 Pattern cars and one (chassis No. 30 PG) which appears to have been from a

Irish Army car *Eleanor* having a wheel changed in Dublin and attracting an interested audience. Notice that the unditching planks are stowed vertically and a Hotchkiss machine gun is mounted at the back of the turret. Note also how the bonnet panels have been chained down and padlocked.

This much modified 1914 Pattern body, on a new chassis fitted with heavy-duty tyres was operated by the Calcutta and Presidency Battalion, part of the Indian Auxiliary Force staffed mostly by Europeans. The markings appear to follow British practice and the symbol on the near wing seems to be that of the 303rd (Bengal) Lines of Communication Area. Markhor is a local species of wild goat.

conventional Silver Ghost car to which an armoured body was fitted during World War II when the original chassis wore out. They were involved in the Irish Civil War and one car, chassis No. 103 WO, *Slievenamon* (*Sliabh na mBan*), was reputedly escorting Michael Collins, head of the Provisional Government, when he was ambushed and killed in August 1922. That car still survives at the Curragh.

All 13 Rolls-Royces were still in service towards the end of World War II, by which time a shortage of tyres was becoming critical and attempts to replace the original Michelin wheel rims with those from a Morris lorry also failed. As a result, all of these cars except for 103 WO were stripped of their armour and the chassis sold off to private buyers.

Mention should also be made of the near legendary Moon Car, a yellow-painted tourer fitted with two Lewis guns that was operated briefly by the IRA before being dumped in a bog. It was not armoured, nor was it technically

Privately owned Rolls-Royce armoured cars are a rarity but this one is reputed to have been built to the order of an Indian nobleman who planned to use it on hunting expeditions. Whether he did or not is impossible to say, although the car itself reportedly still survives, blocked up on bricks in its garage but still apparently more or less complete.

A Silver Ghost chassis set up as an instructional model in the Drill Hall of the 26th Armoured Car Company (East Riding Yeomanry) at Hull. Had it not been for the outbreak of World War II this might have been the ultimate role for Rolls-Royce armoured cars in the British Army.

a military vehicle, but it was an armed Silver Ghost. It has since been recovered and is undergoing restoration.

India

One comment, attributed to the Viceroy, Lord Hardinge, and apparently uttered to Lord Montague concerning armoured cars, was that they might get 'some of those... that Winston Churchill so recklessly bought'. About a year later the War Office promised to deliver a dozen turreted Rolls-Royces, which would originally have been Royal Naval Air Service cars from Churchill's time, but they never came. Instead six were shipped to India from the Middle East, three at a time starting in 1917. These ultimately formed Nos. 2 and 3 Armoured Motor Batteries operating on the Frontier alongside Clifton's original three improvised Rolls-Royces.

At the end of the war more of these cars followed and, by 1921, had been formed into Armoured Car Companies of the Tank Corps, which slowly grew in number over the next few years. At least one of these, the 7th Armoured Car Company, operated Rolls-Royces of the 1914 turreted Pattern, although they had been modified in a number of ways to suit local conditions. Virtually all

 ROLLS-ROYCE 1920 PATTERN MARK I, IRISH CAVALRY CORPS, NEAR BLARNEY, 1941

The Irish Army received 13 Rolls-Royce armoured cars and various other vehicles from the British Government in 1922 following the creation of the Irish Free State. In the Irish Army they were known as Whippets, although how their engineers managed to keep them going for so long, with a limited range of spares, is something of a mystery. They lasted until the end of World War II, during which they were employed on home defence duties although by then the supply of new tyres was becoming chronic. The car is finished in a two-tone disruptive scheme of dark and light grey. Generally speaking it seems that the cars in Ireland were more original, having undergone fewer modifications and improvements than their British counterparts.

Although it was a neutral country, Ireland felt that it was vulnerable, on account of its position, from both Germany and Great Britain, and consequently maintained an active defence force. However, as may be seen, the British practice of removing road signs to confuse an invader was not followed in Ireland.

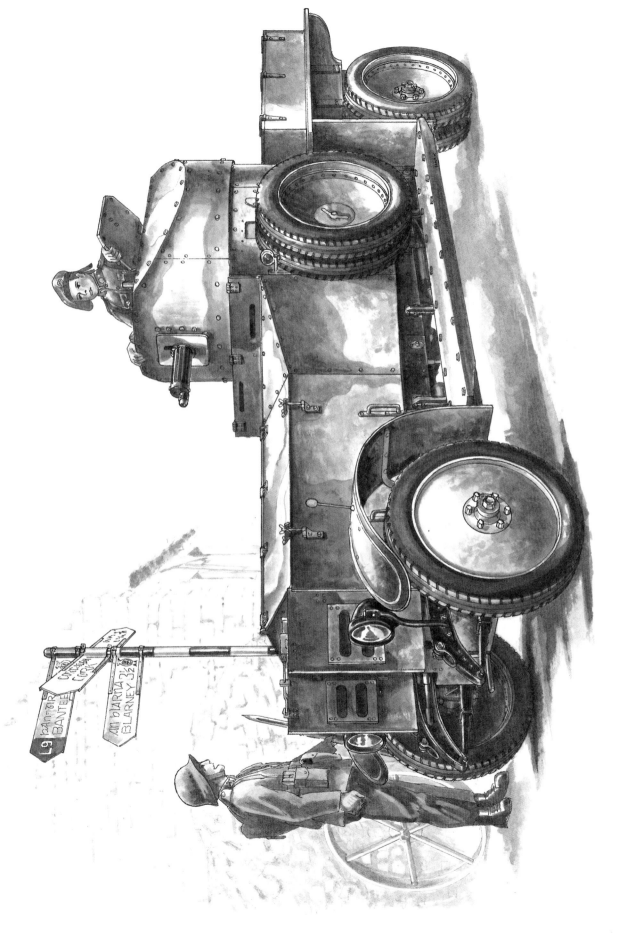

were fitted with steel disc wheels and shod with MacIntosh Normal Air Pressure (NAP) tyres, which were effectively solid and therefore unpuncturable, but very narrow and quite lethal on a slippery surface. Many cars also had protected loopholes cut into the bevelled plates of the turret to enable the crew to use rifles against tribal marksmen in the passes in an ambush situation. Some were fitted with spotlights on top of the turret for use at night.

Meanwhile Clifton had been sent back to Britain in 1920 to examine and help design a new generation of Rolls-Royce armoured cars for India. The need for them had been agreed by the authorities in India and the War Office in London and, based on previous experience, the Rolls-Royce Silver Ghost chassis was considered to be the ideal. But things had changed since 1914; prices had risen and makers of luxury automobiles had customers waiting in line to acquire new cars with their wartime fortunes – blood money Clifton would have called it.

A Silver Ghost chassis, prepared for military use, was quoted at £2,100, a small fortune at that time, and that was without armour or weapons. The most that Clifton could afford was 19 cars, enough to equip one of the new companies, and although Rolls-Royce were in no hurry to accept the deal – they already had 100 chassis on order from the War Office and an impatient civilian clientele – the new cars were steadily delivered. Meanwhile Clifton, in conjunction with a design team from Vickers Ltd, was working on the body with a prototype constructed on a spare chassis. Clifton was particularly keen to have a fully enclosed body, lined with a patent asbestos-based material know as Raybestos to reduce the heat, and surmounted by a large, dome-shaped turret with optional machine-gun mountings capable of high elevation for use in the narrow passes of the North West Frontier. Construction of the bodies was undertaken by Vickers at their Erith works in Kent, under the control of one of their senior designers, Sir George Buckham.

In May 1921 a challenging hill-climbing trial was organized at Leith Hill, on the North Downs in Surrey, a favourite site for military trials on account of

Two or three Rolls-Royce armoured cars, virtually identical to those built for India, were supplied to the government of Iran. The most obvious difference was the use of pneumatic tyres, which required spares, two of which can be seen mounted on the left side of this vehicle.

its supposed similarity to the Indian Frontier. Rolls-Royce condescended to enter two of their new chassis, which they expected would show the other contestants up, particularly since they insisted upon employing their own drivers. The trial was an abject failure for Rolls-Royce, inducing serious mortification amongst the observers. Clifton blamed the choice of gear ratios but Sir Henry Royce preferred the idea of an epicyclic rear axle with an emergency low gear but calculated a price increase of £600 per chassis, which the authorities in India refused to pay. Others consider that the use of narrow NAP tyres, which Clifton had insisted upon, may have been the cause. MacIntosh had been reluctant to supply them for such heavy vehicles but Clifton managed to persuade them to come up with a more substantial version.

These cars arrived in India in September 1922 and were issued exclusively to the 9th Armoured Car Company of what was then, still, the Tank Corps. Within a month they had moved to the North West Frontier where one section was involved in the Chitral Relief Column.

The 1924 Pattern cars

The prototype of a new style of armoured body on the Silver Ghost appeared in 1925 and was tested on a long-distance road run from Bovington to Cardiff. It was probably more of a pilot model than a prototype since the running chassis was a known quantity and it was only the design of body and turret that was new. The car was photographed in Pontypridd, South Wales on 27 March 1925 and appeared in the local paper, the *Western Mail*, the following day. Included in the photograph was Colonel George Lindsay, described as Chief Instructor Central Schools, Royal Tank Corps Centre at Bovington, who was travelling in the car as part of the crew. One of Lindsay's brothers was Chief Constable of Glamorgan and the stop at Pontypridd was to show him the new car.

The pilot for the 1924 Pattern cars somewhat overwhelmed by Royal Tank Corps personnel in overalls of various shades. It can be distinguished from production cars by the way the armour is carried all the way to the rear of the chassis.

39

A 1924 Pattern armoured car taking part in a funeral at Bovington Camp, passing Smiths Restaurant. The machine gun is dipped but the headlamps have not been reversed, which was normal practice for a military funeral.

The newspaper went on to say that the true purpose of the visit was to try the car on some of the more difficult roads in the mountains around the Rhondda Valley since they were reckoned to be, topographically, very similar to the North West Frontier of India, although in fact this type of armoured car never saw service in India.

The new car was quite distinctive: still recognizably a Rolls-Royce of course and very similar at the front end to the earlier 1920 Pattern, but further back it was quite different. For a start, the armoured body was carried all the way to the back of the chassis, with a large access door on the left side, while the turret was a cylindrical affair, with a bevel at the front and a full-width cupola mounted crosswise. The machine gun was carried in the front of the turret in a lockable ball mounting.

The production model was known officially as the Rolls-Royce Armoured Car 1924 Pattern Mark I, although there is no evidence that there was ever a Mark II. It followed the general lines of the pilot model, except at the rear where the armoured hull was reduced in length and replaced by an open wooden tray with a short tailgate and what are described as wooden chests on each side. And all this presumably to save weight.

Twenty-four cars of this type were supplied, with the last three chassis coming from Rolls-Royce to a contract dated 1927. Bearing in mind that Silver Ghost production ended in 1924 in favour of the new Phantom model of the following year, this suggests that Rolls-Royce retained an interest in the requirements of their military customer.

The majority of these cars were shipped out to Egypt, where they were issued, in the first place, to 3rd Armoured Car Company, Royal Tank Corps. They were used on a number of excursions into the desert but, being that much heavier than the 1920 Pattern, did not perform so well on soft sand.

The establishment of an Armoured Car Company at this time was 16 cars, the company being divided into four sections of four cars each. By November 1927 3rd Armoured Car Company was complete to establishment with 1924 Pattern cars having returned its entire 1920 Pattern fleet to Britain. However, in January of 1929 3rd Armoured Car Company handed over 11 of its cars to the newly mechanized 12th Royal Lancers, who they had already been training for their new role.

To begin with it was B Squadron 12th Lancers who gave up their horses for armoured cars; the squadron comprised two sections of five cars each, and one extra car for the squadron leader. By September 1930 all three squadrons and headquarters had converted although by that time B Squadron had already seen some action in Palestine. Of course, not all of these were 1924 Pattern cars and the regiment was very complimentary about the quality, if not their performance over soft sand. Their regimental history states: 'Until fitted with sand-tyres, for the development of which the Regiment was largely responsible, they tended to dig themselves in in a big way...' but quite what this means is unclear.

In 1934 the War Office issued a new War Establishment for a cavalry armoured car regiment with a total of 38 cars of which the three squadrons had three troops each of three cars, plus three cars at each squadron headquarters and two more at regimental headquarters. The 12th Lancers reported that the three-car troop was a lot easier to handle.

Their most famous exploit at this time – the summer of 1932 – was a motorized expedition by A Squadron with ten armoured cars and an assortment of transport vehicles from Helmieh, near Cairo, to the legendary Siwa Oasis, deep in the Libyan Desert via Mersah Matruh and Sollum. The event was recorded by their doctor, Major T.I. Dun, RAMC, in a lavish publication entitled *From Cairo to Siwa Across the Libyan Desert with Armoured Cars.*

A 1924 Pattern car in service with the 11th Hussars in Palestine in 1936. Experience serving alongside Royal Air Force armoured cars caused the regiment to remove the cupola from the turret and fit a spare Lewis gun instead. However this car is fitted for radio, which is not usual in a Rolls-Royce and has what appear to be ranging poles stowed at the front.

The distinctive domed turret and enlarged body of an Indian Pattern armoured car. One is tempted to suggest that the name on this car was intended as a joke, although Barasingha are a breed of native deer. Even so with the engine armour removed one can see clearly that it is a Rolls-Royce. Notice the steel disc wheels and the narrow, solid NAP tyres.

The 11th Hussars replaced the 12th Lancers in Egypt in November 1934 and after a year of relatively peaceful training in the desert found themselves bound for Palestine around Easter 1936 to maintain the peace between Jews and Arabs, which at this remove may be seen as a foretaste of World War II. The three squadrons were stationed in different parts of the country and often had detached sections either patrolling the roads or covering known trouble spots.

They were not the only armoured units in Palestine; C Squadron of 6th Royal Tank Corps was there with some light tanks along with No. 2 Armoured Car Company Royal Air Force, who also had Rolls-Royces. Indeed the 11th Hussars were so impressed by the RAF practice of attaching an extra machine gun, usually a Lewis gun, to the top of the turret that they followed suit, often removing the cupolas from their 1924 Pattern cars at the same time.

Four wheels good – six wheels better

In 1926 the War Office became convinced that for load-carrying across country a six-wheeled vehicle offered far greater potential than a four-wheeler and before long the majority of army lorries in the 30cwt and 3-ton payload classes were in this category, mostly employing the special War Department articulating rear bogie. It was not long before this idea was extended to

Even so some of the older cars survived; this one was photographed with a formal group of 2nd Armoured Car Company at Cawnpore in 1931. Features to note are the stylish new front mudguards, the ventilation slots in the radiator doors and the armoured shield over the machine-gun aperture.

armoured cars. However, Rolls-Royce would have none of it; one tampered with their handiwork at one's peril. Even so there was a six-wheeled Silver Ghost, created by a small bus company in Wiltshire using a pair of redundant Rolls-Royce armoured car back axles and one feels that what they could achieve in a small shed on Salisbury Plain an organization such as Royal Ordnance could do a lot better, with or without the sanction of Derby, or indeed Royce himself. In the event it was never done and the War Office turned to other firms to provide their armoured six-wheelers. Indeed the closest we come to a six-wheeled Rolls-Royce was in India, where the armoured body of a Rolls-Royce was fitted to a Morris-Commercial 6x4 chassis as an experiment. Since no detailed report or photograph has yet been found we do not know whether the car concerned was one of the surviving Admiralty type or a dome-turreted Indian Pattern car and in any case without its original chassis it was not a Rolls-Royce anyway – it just looked like one.

WORLD WAR II

Apart from the special Home Guard vehicles mentioned below, the role of Rolls-Royce armoured cars in World War II was a rapidly diminishing one. The most active were the 11th Hussars (the Cherrypickers) in Egypt, who now had their surviving cars modified, replacing the turret with an open box and the original armament with a Bren gun, Boys anti-tank rifle and a 4-inch smoke grenade discharger. These cars were already up on the frontier with Libya when the war with Italy broke out and in no time at all were creating gaps in the Italian wire and harassing their border forts. They held their own against the Italians to begin with but suffered badly at the hands of the Italian Air Force until the surviving cars were withdrawn and replaced by South African-built Marmon-Herringtons. Also it is worth remarking that elements of No. 2 Armoured Car Company RAF formed a temporary D Squadron to

This Rolls-Royce, followed by two Peerless armoured cars, is apparently on airfield defence duties 'somewhere in Britain', operated by the Derbyshire Yeomanry. It is being overflown by an early P-51 Mustang fighter.

the 11th Hussars although by this time most of their armoured cars were running on Fordson chassis.

The Irish Army managed to maintain their Rolls-Royces for the duration of the war, mainly on home defence duties but the supply of spare tyres was almost exhausted and attempts to find replacement wheels failed. All but one of these cars were sold off after the war, once the armour had been removed, to private buyers to reappear as private cars in due course. The North Irish Horse, the last surviving Militia regiment, was reconstituted as a Light Armoured Regiment (wheeled) on 31 August 1939 and initially received about a dozen 1920 Pattern Rolls-Royces from British Army stocks. Later, the regiment retrained to operate Churchill tanks.

It is interesting that when the 12th Lancers went to France with the British Expeditionary Force they were equipped entirely with Morris armoured vehicles and no Rolls-Royces, unlike their sister regiment the 11th Hussars in the Middle East. Those Rolls-Royces still in Britain were largely in the hands of mobilized Yeomanry regiments undertaking internal security patrols, pending the delivery of tanks. Some found themselves patrolling the sands of the East Coast beaches, much as their forebears had done on anti-invasion duties in 1915.

G

1. MODIFIED ROLLS-ROYCE 1924 PATTERN MARK I, NEAR BARDIA, 11 JUNE 1940

The 11th (Prince Albert's Own) Hussars, otherwise known as the Cherrypickers, had been operating in armoured cars since 1928. Many were from the final batch, the 1924 Pattern, but even these were becoming quite long in the tooth by 1939. Even so by then some of them had been fitted with a new, open-top turret that shared the same armament as the newer Morris armoured cars that were supposed to replace them; that is to say a Bren gun, a Boys anti-tank rifle and a 4-inch smoke bomb discharger. The conversion was carried out by the Nairn Transport Company at their workshops in Cairo. This new turret did not rotate but that did not matter so much since the weapons were more flexible. It was, for example, possible to mount the Bren gun at the rear for anti-aircraft use although early experience against Italian aircraft in the desert indicated that the 28-round upright magazine supplied with the Bren was not really adequate for this role.

The car is finished in a basic sand shade with a disruptive pattern in a darkish red, like primer. There is a lot of interesting detail in this illustration. Notice for instance the sun compass on the lip of the turret above the smoke discharger, the steel sand channel on the side – although the Rolls-Royce still retains the undicthing board beneath the running board – and the canvas bucket hanging at the back.

The cap badge of the 11th Hussars is shown although by tradition and royal decree it would not be attached to the beret. The crew wear a light-brown beret with a red band at the bottom and this was considered so distinctive that their Colonel-in-Chief, His Majesty King George VI, announced that a badge would be superfluous.

2. PRIVATELY BUILT ROLLS-ROYCE ARMOURED CAR OF THE 47TH BATTALION LONDON COUNTY COUNCIL HOME GUARD, LONDON, 1940

There were two battalions of the London County Council (LCC) Home Guard raised entirely from LCC staff and one of them operated this impressive armoured car. It was based on the chassis of a 1930 Rolls-Royce, probably a Phantom, which was donated by the Chairman of the LCC.

The armour, such as it was, usually amounted to steel plate no more than 6mm thick and hardly even bulletproof although the .303-inch Vickers machine gun in the turret was real enough. Cooling air for the radiator must have been drawn in under the armour since there is no grille or doors at the front, but notice the hinged panels on the wheel covers, which would come in handy if it was necessary to change a wheel. The battalion operated an armoured car of similar appearance on a 1936 Standard chassis and both were photographed extensively on exercises with other Home Guard detachments in London.

The other markings are the yellow-on-khaki shoulder title of the Home Guard and the fabric patch indicating a London battalion.

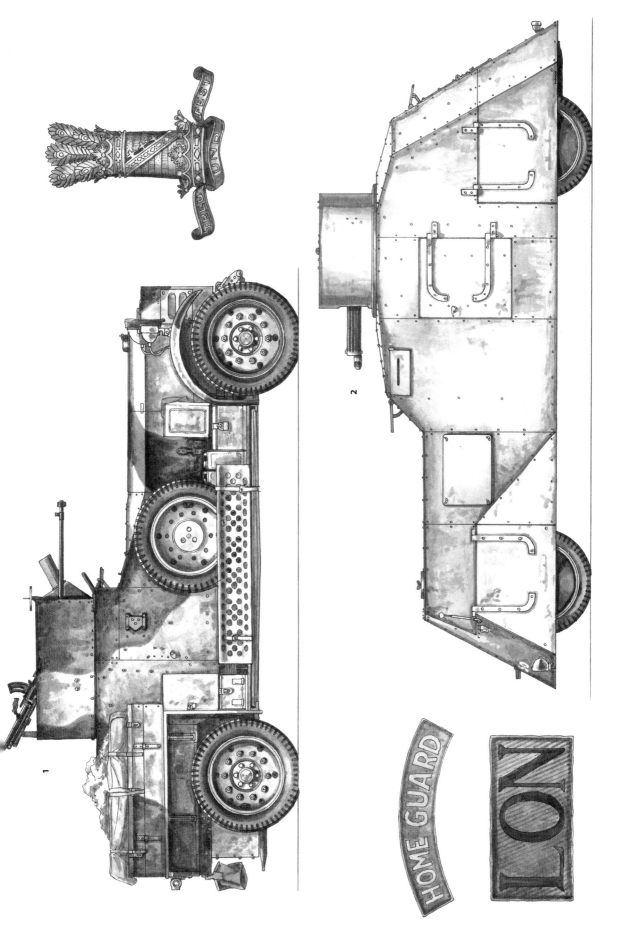

1

2

TREU UND FEST

HOME GUARD

ION

A 1920 Pattern Mark I car in service with the North Irish Horse in Ulster, early in World War II. The turret is reversed but a ball mounting for a Hotchkiss gun is fitted into the rear hatch. The unditching planks appear to be missing and the car commander is wearing a steel helmet. Notice that by this stage armoured cars had the prefix F to their War Department numbers where previously it had been M.

The Home Guard

Affectionately ridiculed as Dad's Army, because many of its personnel were veterans of World War I and had the medal ribbons to prove it, the Home Guard was taken seriously in the early days and, as if to establish their modern credentials, many units acquired at least one armoured vehicle, much as some Yeomanry regiments had in the earlier war.

All were essentially home-made to whatever design took the units' fancy although the majority offered their crew very little protection and some designs were positively bizarre. None of them were officially recognized by the War Office and in some cases units were actively discouraged from acquiring them. Even so some were armed with machine guns, which suggests a degree of official connivance. Of those for which information survives at least three are known to have been created on Rolls-Royce chassis.

One such, operated by the 29th (East Lancashire) Battalion based in Burnley must have been a Silver Ghost if the claim that it was constructed at the local bus garage on a 20-year-old chassis that had once been a hearse is true. It was covered in quarter-inch plate, had seating for six men inside and was armed with a stripped Lewis gun in a small turret.

The 53rd (Orpington & Swanley) Battalion in Kent also built their car on a Rolls-Royce chassis but there are no clues as to what type. The body was reputedly fabricated from scrap metal, and looks like it. It also carried a stripped Lewis gun, this time in a box-shaped structure on top of the body, which presumably did not rotate.

Finally an altogether more professional-looking design was that fielded by a Battalion of the London County Council Home Guard and reputedly donated by the Chairman of the LCC. It forms the subject of the final colour illustration and is described in more detail in the related commentary.

BIBLIOGRAPHY

Anon., *Rolls-Royce and the Great Victory*, Bronte-Hill Publications (1972)

Bird, Anthony and Hallows, Ian, *The Rolls-Royce Motor Car*, Batsford (1984)

Dun, Major T.I., *From Cairo to Siwa Across the Libyan Desert with Armoured Cars*, E & R Schindler, Cairo (1933)

Fasal, John and Goodman, Bryan, *The Edwardian Rolls-Royce*, John Fasal (1994)

Fletcher, David, *War Cars*, HMSO (1987)

Kautt, W.H., *Ambushes and Armour, the Irish Rebellion 1919–1921*, Irish Academic Press (2010)

Kutz, Captain C.R., *War on Wheels*, Military Service Publishing (1940)

Martin, Karl, *Irish Army Vehicles*, Karl Martin (2002)

Myers, A. Wallis, *Captain Anthony Wilding*, Hodder & Stoughton (1917)

Raleigh, Walter, *The War in the Air Vol. 1*, Clarendon Press (1922)

Rolls, S.C., *Steel Chariots in the Desert*, Rolls-Royce Enthusiasts Club (1988)

Roosevelt, Kermit, *War in the Garden of Eden*, Charles Scribner (1919)

Samson, Air-Commodore Charles Rumney, *Fights and Flights*, Ernest Benn Ltd (1930)

Sueter, Rear Admiral Sir Murray, *The Evolution of the Tank*, Hutchinson & Co. (1937)

White, B.T., *British Tanks and Fighting Vehicles 1914–1945*, Ian Allan (1970)

Whittall, W., *With Botha and Smuts in Africa*, Cassell (1917)

Winstone, H.V.F., *Leachman O. C. Desert*, Quartet Books (1982)

Said to be a Rolls-Royce belonging to the 29th (East Lancashire) Battalion Home Guard in Burnley it is believed to have used the chassis of a Silver Ghost that had latterly been used as a hearse; the body and turret are reputed to have been fitted at the local bus garage.

INDEX

Illustrations are referred to in **bold.** For plates the page number is in bold followed by the caption locator in brackets - eg. **39** (38)

1914 Pattern cars **21** (20), **23**, 26, **30**, 36, 38
1914/1920 hybrid 30, **31**, **35**
1920 Pattern cars
  design 23–7, **24–5**
  Ireland 34–5, 37 (36), 44, **46**
  Mark I **24–5**, 26–7, **37** (36), **46**
  Mark IA 27, **31**
  RAF **29**, 30–1
  service record 27–31, 34–5, **37** (36) 44, **46**
1924 Pattern cars 31, **33** (32), 39–42, **45** (44)

Admiralty 4–5, 6, **6**, **9** (8), 15, 23
Africa 11, **11**, 15–16, 18, **18**, 32, 41 *see also* Egypt
Albuera, HMAC **33** (32)
armour plate 4–5, 6, **9** (8), 10–11, **21** (20), **24–5**, **45** (44)
Arras, Battle of (1917) 13, **13**, **17** (16)

brakes 10, **24–5**, **26**
British Army
  1/6th (Cyclists Battalion) 12
  1st Armoured Car Company, Tank Corps 14
  1st Armoured Motor Battery 20
  2nd Armoured Car Company, Tank Corps **42**
  3rd Armoured Car Company, Royal Tank Corps 40–1
  3rd Battalion Royal Tank Corps 27–8
  5th Armoured Car Company, Royal Tank Corps 28–9, **29**, 34
  6th Light Armoured Motor Battery **19**, 23
  7th Armoured Car Company **23**
  9th Armoured Car Company, Royal Tank Corps **33** (32)
  11th Hussars 31, 32, **41**, 42, 43–4, **45** (44)
  12th Armoured Car Company 27, 34
  12th Lancers 29, **33** (32), 41, 44
  13th LAMB 18
  14th LAMB 18
  15th LAMB **14**, 18–19
  17th (Armoured Car) Battalion, Tank Corps 32, 34
  Hedjaz Armoured Car Section 16, **18**
  Light Armoured Car Brigade 16
  Machine Gun Corps (Motors) 12–13, **17** (16)
  No.1 Armoured Motor Unit **21** (20), 22
  No.1 Squadron 5–6, 15
  No.2 Armoured Car Company, RAF 18, **21** (20), 31, 32, 42, 43–4
  No.2 Squadron 12
  North Irish Horse 44, **46**
  North Persia Force **14**, 18–19
  RAF **14**, **21** (20), **29**, 30–2, 42
  Shanghai Defence Force 28–9
  see also Home Guard; Yeomanry

camouflage 13, **17** (16), **19**, **21** (20), **33** (32), **45** (44)
chassis
  1920 Pattern **24–5**, 31, 34–5
  1924 Pattern 40
  continual change 7, 20, 22
  Fordson **21** (20), 31, 44
  hybrid (1914/1920) 30, **31**, **35**
  M350 **28**
  Phantom **45** (44)
  Silver Ghost 8, **9** (8), 10, **33** (32), 34–6, **36**, 38–9, 40, 46, **47**
  six-wheeled 42–3

Chatham, HMAC **14**
Cheetah, HMAC **21** (20)
China 28–9, **29**
Churchill, Winston 4–5, **6**
Clifton, Captain Anthony 19–23, **21** (20), **33** (32), 38–9
crew compartment 5, 6, **6**, 11, **24–5**, 31

deserts, cars in **10**, **11**, 15–16, **17** (16), 18, **18**, 31, **33** (32), 40–1
drivers 5, 10–11, 18, **24–5**, 26, **26**, 27
Duff, Morgan and Vermont 23, 26

Egypt 15, 28, **28**, **29**, **33** (32), 40–2, 43
Eleanor (Irish Army car) **34**
engine 8, 10–11, **24–5**, 27

fighting compartment **10**, **11**
First Admiralty Pattern car **9** (8)
Flanders 5, **9** (8), 12, 15
France 5, 12–13, 15, 44
fuel pumps 10, **24–5**

Gallipoli 14–15
gears 7, 8, 10, **24–5**, **26**, 39
Guillemont, Battle of (1916) 13
gun carriages 6, 12, **13**

Hardinge, Lord 36
Home Guard **45** (44), 46

ignition system 10, **24–5**, **26**
India 19–23, **33** (32), 35, 36–9
Indian Pattern car **22**, **33** (32), **42**
Iraq **21** (20), 29, 30
Ireland 32, 34–6, **37** (36), 44
Italy 43

Lawrence, Colonel T.E. (Lawrence of Arabia) 16, 18, 30
Lindsay, Lieutenant-Colonel George 30, 39
Locker-Lampson, Oliver 26
London County Council Home Guard **45** (44)
lorries, armoured 12

machine-gun mountings 5, 11, 22, **24–5**, **33** (32) 38 *see also* weapons
Middle East **14**, **17** (16), 18–19, **21** (20), 28, 29–31, **38**, 41, 42
Montague, Lord (John) of Beaulieu 20
Moon Car 35–6
mudguards 26

Nickerson, Arthur **6**
North West Frontier 20, 22, **23**, **33** (32), 38, 39

Pathfinder **30**
Phantoms 27, 40, **45** (44)
pneumatic tyres 10, **24–5**, **33** (32), 38, **38**, 39, **42**
Pontypridd 39–40
privately owned cars 4, 35, **35**, 44
Python, HMAC **31**

radiators 5, **5**, 10, **24–5**, 26, 27, **45** (44)
Rolls-Royce (company) 38–9, 40, 43
Rolls, Sam **11**, 12, 18
Royal Naval Air Service (RNAS) 4–5, **9** (8), 12
Royal Naval Armoured Car Division (RNACD) 7, 12, 15

Royce, Sir Henry 39
Russia 14, 18–19, 26

Samson, Commander Charles 4–6, 12, 13, 15
Samson, Felix 4, **5**
Silver Ghost 8, **9** (8), 10, **33** (32), 34–6, **36**, 38–9, 40, 43, 46, **47**
six-wheeled cars 42–3
Stern, Lieutenant, A.G. 15
Sueter, Commodore Murray 4–5
suspension 10

tanks, and armoured cars 13, 28, 31
Trenchard, Sir Hugh 30
trials, hill-climbing 38–3
turrets
  1914 Pattern cars **9** (8), **21** (20), **23**, **30**, **31**
  1920 Pattern cars **24–5**, **26**, 27, **27**, **29**, **31**
  1924 Pattern cars 39, 40, **45** (44)
  cupolas **17** (16), 27, **29**, **31**, **33** (32), 40, **41**
  in the desert **11**, **17** (16)
  dome-shaped **33** (32), 38, **42**
  early designs 6–7
  enlarged **19**, 23, 26
  general design 11
  Indian cars **22**, **33** (32)
  modifications 22, 23, 43, **45** (46), **46**
  World War I 13, **17** (16)
tyres
  deserts 31, **31**, 41
  heavy duty **35**
  pneumatic 10, **24–5**, **33** (32), 38, **38**, 39, **42**
  protection of 5, 11
  shortages of 35, 44
  spare **17** (16), **18**, 38, 44

Uralite 13, **17** (16)

Vickers Ltd 38

War Office 12, 23, 26–7, 36, 38, 41, 42–3
weapons
  Boys anti-tank rifles 32, 43, **45** (44)
  Bren guns 43, **45** (44)
  Hotchkiss guns **34**, 46
  Lewis guns **21** (20), **29**, 31, 35, 42, 46
  machine guns, scarcity in India 22
  Maxim guns 4, 5, **9** (8), 11, **21** (20)
  rifles **9** (8), 32, 38
  Vickers guns 7, 11, **24–5**, 27, **27**, 31, 32, **33** (32), **45** (44)
Wedding Bells 22–3, **22**
Western Mail 39–40
Westminster, Duke of 12, 16
wheels 10–11, **24–5**, 26, 28, 38, **42**, 42–3
Whittall, Lieutenant-Commander W. 15
Wilding, Anthony Lieutenant 12
World War I
  Admiralty to army control 12–13, 15
  Africa 15–16, 18, **18**
  Europe **9** (8), 12–13, 15, **17** (16)
  Gallipoli 14–15
  India 19–20, **21** (20), 22–3, **22**
  Middle East 14–15, **17** (16), **18**, **19**, **21** (20)
  Russia **14**, 18–19
  Yeomanry **19**, **19**
World War II 43–6

Yeomanry **19**, **19**, 27, **43**, 44
Ypres **9** (8), 12